I0763447

Published by Angelis Publications
ISBN: 978-1-912484-22-5
www.angelispublications.com

In Loving Memory of

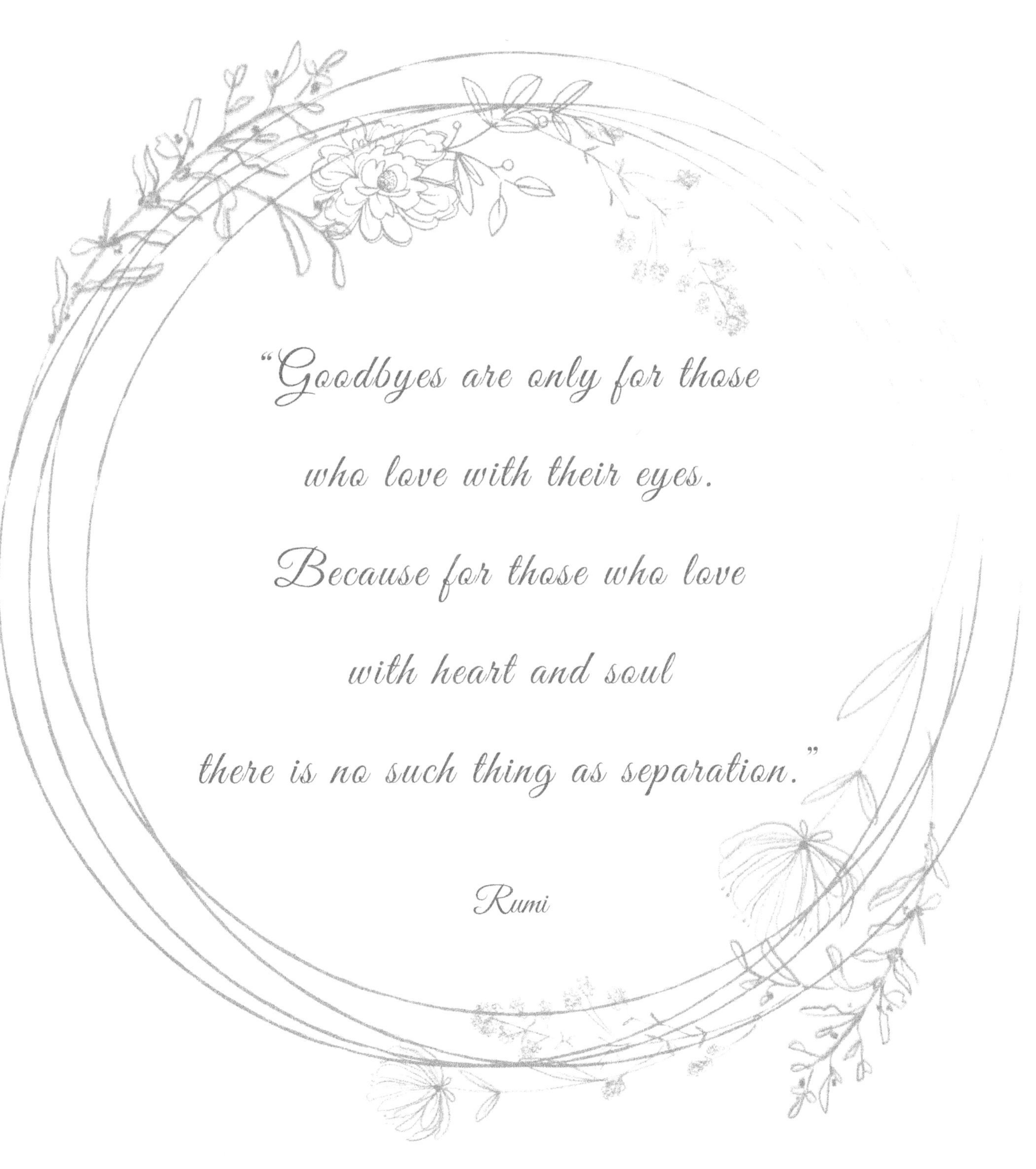

"Goodbyes are only for those
who love with their eyes.
Because for those who love
with heart and soul
there is no such thing as separation."

Rumi

Name / Address

Thoughts & Memories

Name / Address

Thoughts & Memories

Name / Address

Thoughts & Memories

Name / Address

Thoughts & Memories

Name / Address

Thoughts & Memories

Name / Address

Thoughts & Memories

Name / Address

Thoughts & Memories

Name / Address

Thoughts & Memories

Name / Address

Thoughts & Memories

Name / Address

Thoughts & Memories

Name / Address

Thoughts & Memories

Name / Address

Thoughts & Memories

Name / Address

Thoughts & Memories

Name / Address

Thoughts & Memories

Name / Address

Thoughts & Memories

Name / Address

Thoughts & Memories

Name / Address

Thoughts & Memories

Name / Address

Thoughts & Memories

Name / Address

Thoughts & Memories

Name / Address

Thoughts & Memories

Name / Address

Thoughts & Memories

Name / Address

Thoughts & Memories

Name / Address

Thoughts & Memories

Name / Address

Thoughts & Memories

Name / Address

Thoughts & Memories

Name / Address

Thoughts & Memories

Name / Address

Thoughts & Memories

Name / Address

Thoughts & Memories

Name / Address

Thoughts & Memories

Name / Address

Thoughts & Memories

Name / Address

Thoughts & Memories

Name / Address

Thoughts & Memories

Name / Address

Thoughts & Memories

Name / Address

Thoughts & Memories

Name / Address

Thoughts & Memories

Name / Address

Thoughts & Memories

Name / Address

Thoughts & Memories

Name / Address

Thoughts & Memories

Name / Address

Thoughts & Memories

Name / Address

Thoughts & Memories

Name / Address

Thoughts & Memories

Name / Address

Thoughts & Memories

Name / Address

Thoughts & Memories

Name / Address

Thoughts & Memories

Name / Address

Thoughts & Memories

Name / Address

Thoughts & Memories

Name / Address

Thoughts & Memories

Name / Address

Thoughts & Memories

Name / Address

Thoughts & Memories

Name / Address

Thoughts & Memories

Name / Address

Thoughts & Memories

Name / Address

Thoughts & Memories

Name / Address

Thoughts & Memories

Name / Address

Thoughts & Memories

Name / Address

Thoughts & Memories

Name / Address

Thoughts & Memories

Name / Address

Thoughts & Memories

Name / Address

Thoughts & Memories

Name / Address

Thoughts & Memories

Name / Address

Thoughts & Memories

Name / Address

Thoughts & Memories

Name / Address

Thoughts & Memories

Name / Address

Thoughts & Memories

Name / Address

Thoughts & Memories

Name / Address

Thoughts & Memories

Name / Address

Thoughts & Memories

Name / Address

Thoughts & Memories

Name / Address

Thoughts & Memories

Name / Address

Thoughts & Memories

Name / Address

Thoughts & Memories

Name / Address

Thoughts & Memories

Name / Address

Thoughts & Memories

Name / Address

Thoughts & Memories

Name / Address

Thoughts & Memories

Name / Address

Thoughts & Memories

Name / Address

Thoughts & Memories

Name / Address

Thoughts & Memories

Name / Address

Thoughts & Memories

Name / Address

Thoughts & Memories

Name / Address

Thoughts & Memories

Name / Address

Thoughts & Memories

Name / Address

Thoughts & Memories

Name / Address

Thoughts & Memories

Name / Address

Thoughts & Memories

Name / Address

Thoughts & Memories

Name / Address

Thoughts & Memories

Name / Address

Thoughts & Memories

Name / Address

Thoughts & Memories

Name / Address

Thoughts & Memories

Name / Address

Thoughts & Memories

Name / Address

Thoughts & Memories

Name / Address

Thoughts & Memories

Name / Address

Thoughts & Memories

Name / Address

Thoughts & Memories

www.ingramcontent.com/pod-product-compliance
Lightning Source LLC
Chambersburg PA
CBHW080809020826
48982CB00016B/859

9781912484225